PATRICK HENRY

DIANA REISCHE

PATRICK HENRY

FRANKLIN WATTS
NEW YORK / LONDON / TORONTO / SYDNEY
A FIRST BOOK / 1987

Cover photograph courtesy of The Granger Collection, New York.

Photographs courtesy of: The Collections of the Library of Congress:
pp. 10, 13, 53, 58, 65, 71, 80, 81; State Historical Society of Wisconsin:
p. 22; Virginia Historical Society: pp. 32, 62; Commonwealth of Virginia,
Virginia State Library: pp. 36, 42, 50, 51, 70, 73.

Library of Congress Cataloging-in-Publication Data
Reische, Diana L.
Patrick Henry.
(A First book)
Bibliography: p.
Includes index.
Summary: Presents the life and career of the orator,
lawyer, statesman, and framer of the Bill of Rights.
1. Henry, Patrick, 1736-1799—Juvenile literature.
2. Legislators—United States—Biography—Juvenile
literature. 3. United States. Continental Congress—
Biography—Juvenile literature. 4. United States—
Politics and government—Revolution, 1775-1783—Juvenile
literature. 5. Virginia—Politics and government—
Revolution, 1775-1783—Juvenile literature. [1. Henry,
Patrick, 1736-1799. 2. Legislators] I. Title.
E302.6.H5R27   1987   973.3'092'4 [B]   86-23363
ISBN 0-531-10305-6

CONTENTS

PATRICK HENRY

INTRODUCTION

Even an excellent young law student couldn't be expected to spend all his time studying. Not when the Virginia Assembly was in town, and he could watch laws being made. On a fine May morning in 1765, twenty-two-year-old Thomas Jefferson wasn't at his desk reading.

Instead, he stood in the doorway of the Virginia House of Burgesses, craning his neck to hear what was said inside. He knew the plainly dressed person who rose to speak. He knew that Patrick Henry played the fiddle and liked to dance.

Jefferson had met Patrick Henry at parties over a Christmas vacation. But he had never seen him turn the full force of his personality on a serious idea. Why, Henry was standing there bold as can be. He was saying that Virginia must oppose the Stamp Act just passed by England.

"Treason, treason," someone yelled. Patrick Henry snapped right back, "If this be treason, make the most of

it!" He did not lack courage! A person could be hanged for treason. Henry was saying that Virginians should take a stand against the king of England.

The speech marked Patrick Henry as a leader of those who were tired of British meddling in the colonies. His 1765 speech began the fight against the Stamp Act. From Virginia the fight spread to other colonies.

For the next ten years, Patrick Henry fanned the sparks that flamed into revolution against English rule. He did it with a speaking voice that would have made him a superb actor. Almost none of his great speeches were copied down as he spoke. No true record exists of his exact words. That's how he probably wanted it. He knew that *how* he spoke was just as important as what he said.

Slender, stoop-shouldered, and almost six feet (180 cm) tall, Henry looked very ordinary until he spoke. Then people found themselves staring at his deep-set eyes. Though they were blue, his eyes seemed to turn black when he spoke in public. His lined face was deeply tanned from spending so much time on horseback.

Henry knew how to seize the moment to stir people to action. He had a fine sense of timing. He could tell when caution was needed, and when the time was right for bold new steps. In 1775, the colonies were trying to find the courage for open revolt against England. Henry gave Patriots a rallying cry. "Give me liberty or give me death," he said. People in every colony quoted him.

From 1765 on, the people of Virginia elected Henry to every office he ever wanted. They even elected him to posts he didn't run for. Except for George Washington, Henry was the most popular person in Virginia. Ordinary people liked and trusted him. He listened to them with the same courtesy he gave to rich and powerful people. He could talk people into his way of thinking.

"He has only to say, 'Let this be Law,' " George Washington once wrote of him, "and it is Law."

In 1776, Henry was elected the first governor of the state of Virginia. Under state law, after three terms, he had to step down. Jefferson became the next governor at a time when British troops were invading the state. The former friends became political rivals.

Jefferson felt bitter when Patrick Henry criticized his actions as governor. He spread this bitterness in many letters. Patrick Henry kept few letters or other records. No diaries or other materials in his own words have been found. Since he left few records of his own, a lot of what is known about him comes from other people.

One of the main sources of information has been Jefferson. Yet even Jefferson, who disagreed strongly with Henry so often, wrote of him: "I think he was the best humored man . . . I almost ever knew and the greatest orator that ever lived. [He knew] the human heart. . . ." Jefferson added that this understanding of people and Henry's speaking ability gained him "a degree of popularity with the people at large never perhaps equaled. . . ."

There was one great issue that popularity did not make people vote the way Henry hoped. When a Constitution was written for the United States in 1787, he tried to defeat it. He thought it took too much power from the states. He feared government power and refused to back a Constitu-

Thomas Jefferson

tion that did not have a bill of rights. His stand helped force the passage of the first ten amendments to the Constitution, the Bill of Rights. These amendments protect many freedoms, such as freedom of speech and the right to a trial by jury.

Though he had opposed the Constitution, Henry backed the new government. He could have held several important posts if he had wanted them. President Washington asked him to serve as chief justice or secretary of state. Henry thanked him, but said no. He'd stay in Virginia.

Henry's reputation rests on his fiery speeches, yet he was a quiet, modest man. He was not flamboyant at all, except when he was talking to an audience. A well-known Virginian named Atkinson wrote a letter in 1774 describing Henry:

> . . . A real half Quaker, Patrick Henry—moderate and mild, and in religious matters a saint, but the very devil in Politics—a son of Thunder. A very useful man, a notable American, very stern and steady in his country's cause and at the same time such a fool that I verily believe it would puzzle even a king to buy him off. . . .

Henry was not a Quaker. What the writer meant was that he lived simply and dressed plainly. He was too honest to take money in bribes. Yet he was eager to make money in honest ways, and he made a fortune as a lawyer and landowner.

He was willing to sacrifice it all to fight for liberty. "He left us all far behind," said Jefferson of Henry in the days leading up to the Revolution against England. "He gave the first impulse to the ball of Revolution."

NEXT DOOR
TO THE FRONTIER

— 1 —

Ruts and puddles dotted the red clay road as a horse-drawn gig jolted homeward after church. Sarah Henry kept her eye on the rutted road as she questioned the boy beside her. She had him repeat what the minister had said that morning. Then she asked him to explain the sermon.

Patrick's gaze wandered to the forest's edge as he began to speak hesitantly. Then he seemed to gain confidence. The lanky twelve year old quoted almost word for word whole chunks of the sermon they had heard. He mimicked the pauses and the sound of the minister's voice. And what a voice that was! The Reverend Samuel Davies was just about the best speaker anyone in these parts had ever heard. Listening to him, Patrick Henry could see how a fine speaker could change how people thought about things.

But then, Patrick knew a lot of people who could talk rings around ordinary folk. His mother's family, the Winstons, was full of men and women who could tell a fine tale or talk a person into voting their way on election day. When Patrick's uncle, William "Langloo" Winston, told of living among Indians, people stopped what they were doing to listen spellbound. Several of Patrick's eight younger sisters also had the Winston bent for independent thinking and gifted speaking.

Patrick didn't quote the Reverend Davies at home. Parson Davies was a Presbyterian. Patrick's father, John Henry, was a strong Church of England supporter. He didn't hold with those other Protestant groups that were luring people away from the Church of England, or Anglican, services.

Sarah made up her own mind about things. Though her husband went to Anglican services, she joined the Presbyterian church. Patrick made up his own mind, too. He stayed an Anglican, or Episcopalian, all his life. That didn't mean he wouldn't ride quite a few miles to hear a good preacher from some other church though.

People in Virginia's backcountry paid close attention when someone told a good story or preached a powerful sermon. Books were scarce and costly. Many folks couldn't read anyway. They learned by listening. They admired a good talker.

In the Henry family, books were treasured. Sarah Henry was well-educated for a woman of her time, though not nearly as well as her second husband, John Henry. He had gone to college in his native Scotland. When he first arrived in Virginia, John Henry worked for another Scot, John Syme. Colonel Syme owned a plantation called Studley in Hanover County. After Colonel Syme died, his outspoken and attractive widow, Sarah, married John Henry.

The Henry's second son was born at Studley on May 29, 1736. They named him after John's brother, the Reverend Patrick Henry, an Anglican minister. Eight daughters and another son were born after Patrick. The busy household also included Sarah's son, John Syme, Jr., from her first marriage.

Patrick spent most of his childhood at Studley. It was land that only recently had been carved into farms from the wilderness forest. Studley was on the western edge of the Tidewater coastal region. Large tobacco plantations dotted the Tidewater. Wealthy Tidewater planters copied the fancy lifestyle of the English upper classes.

People lived much more simply in western Hanover County. Backcountry farms were scattered thinly among tall stands of uncut forest. Most backwoods people worked small farms. They made or grew most of what they used.

It seemed as if the frontier arrived at Studley when Uncle Langloo Winston showed up in his buckskins after disappearing into the wilderness for months. Langloo taught his nephew how to hunt and track. He showed him how to recognize the calls of birds. And he talked glowingly of the vast and beautiful lands west of the mountains.

Patrick went to school sometimes, always reluctantly. Virginia had no public schools, and tutors were scarce in the backwoods. Patrick went to a tiny country school off and on until he was ten. Then John Henry decided he'd better teach the boy himself. Patrick learned some Greek and Latin, as well as math, the subject he liked best.

John Henry was too busy tending his land to teach Patrick every day. That was more than fine with Patrick. His father loved books and studying, but Patrick most certainly did not. He was bright, no question about that. But he'd much rather fish or hunt or prowl the forest and riverbanks than sit inside trying to understand Greek.

A great deal could be learned by listening to people, and Patrick did that very well. He'd listen to his uncle from Scotland, Parson Henry. The Reverend Patrick Henry stopped often at Studley to talk to his brother. The soft Scots burr in their voices grew thicker as the Henry brothers discussed books. They argued about elections and about Virginia politics. Patrick always listened carefully when they talked of important things. He filed the information in his memory.

Mostly though, Patrick was off canoeing, hunting, fishing, or just daydreaming. His parents worried that he was too idle to make much of himself. Only when he broke a collarbone did he stay inside for long. Then, instead of studying, he played his fiddle and taught himself to play the flute as well.

In 1750 Patrick's half brother, John Syme, Jr., came of age. John Henry thought the young man should have the chance to run Studley plantation without having a stepfather around. So the rest of the family moved to land John Henry owned, a plantation he called Mount Brilliant.

Though only 20 miles (32 km) separated the two farms, it was a long day's trip between them. The two places seemed much further apart, for the land changed sharply. The new place was west of the Fall Line that arcs down Virginia. Along the Fall Line, waterfalls, bluffs, and rapids divided the Piedmont highlands from the Tidewater lowlands. The Fall Line also marked a dividing line between the aristocratic life of the Tidewater region and the plainer style of backwoods living.

For a youth who loved to hunt and fish, Mount Brilliant was perfect. Nearby woods and streams teemed with partridge, duck, geese, deer, wolves, and rabbit. Patrick could fish, swim, or canoe with his new friends. People always liked Patrick. They enjoyed his good humor and the careful way he listened to what others had to say. Just to be around Patrick was fun. The only problem was his father, who began grumbling that Patrick was now old enough to start doing a man's work.

When Patrick was fifteen, his father decided there was no point in wasting good money sending him to college. The boy wasn't a scholar. He sent Patrick to work in a country store to learn a trade.

A year later, John Henry bought a stock of goods including salt and cloth. Then he set up Patrick and his older brother William as storekeepers. Patrick managed the store because William was not very responsible.

Many people dropped in to chat. They did not buy much. Families that had money bought most of their goods further east in Tidewater towns. Poorer farm families had to grow or make most of what they needed. Those who did shop rarely paid cash. Tobacco was used as money all through the colony. The boys also let many people buy on credit.

To pass the time between customers, Patrick read books. Though he was never a heavy reader, he did not forget what he read. He also talked to everyone who came along. Years later he said he had rarely met anyone who could not tell him something he did not already know.

The store failed, but Patrick Henry didn't worry. He was not yet nineteen, and about to get married. His bride was sixteen-year-old Sarah Shelton, daughter of a nearby family of landowners. What did Sarah look like? No one seems to have mentioned that fact. What was she like? That's another mystery.

John Shelton gave his daughter and son-in-law six slaves and a 300-acre (120-ha) farm called Pine Slash. Wearing plain homespun clothes, Henry worked alongside his black slaves, hoeing, picking worms off tobacco plants, and feeding the pigs. An elegant visitor from the Tidewater sniffed that young Henry was not keeping up the family's dignity.

The Henrys' first child, Martha, was born at Pine Slash. Sarah was expecting another when fire destroyed the house in 1757. Patrick sold most of his slaves to raise money to open a new store. The young couple moved in with Sarah's family.

Patrick Henry kept detailed records. He noted every shoe buckle, hairpin, bolt of cloth, and pound of salt sold. He recorded many sales on credit. A storekeeper had to give credit because farmers only got money once a year, when their tobacco crop sold. Then they paid their store debt—*if* the crop was good and *if* they got a decent price for it.

Unfortunately, it was a rotten time to be either a farmer or a storekeeper in Virginia. In 1759 lack of rain destroyed the whole crop. Even successful planters faced ruin. No one had much money to spend in stores.

At the same time, taxes went up because of the French and Indian War. Uncle Langloo Winston went off to fight. So did many of Patrick's friends. They wanted to be sure the western lands did not fall into French hands.

The war set people to thinking about governments, about freedom and patriotism. Henry went to hear the Reverend Samuel Davies preach about courage. Davies praised a young colonel named George Washington who was fighting on the frontier.

The colonists and the English fought on the same side in the French and Indian war. Yet there were many problems between the two groups. The English looked down their noses at colonists. Colonists felt that they were treated badly by English merchants. The English would not let colonists sell their crops to merchants of any country except England. In these hard times, people complained a lot.

Henry was not gloomy about these problems, or the fact that he had to close his second store. He had failed at every job he had tried. Yet he acted as lighthearted as ever. During the 1759 Christmas holidays, he showed up at all the parties, flute or fiddle in hand. He loved to dance, but he was willing to fiddle too so other people could dance.

Another guest at these parties was a tall, sandy-haired teenager from Albemarle County. Tom Jefferson had stopped at the Dandridge's in Hanover on the way to college in Williamsburg. Jefferson was a serious and scholarly youth when he met Henry. He thought the older man was too ready to mix with common people.

"His manners had something of coarseness in them," said Jefferson. "His passion was music, dancing, and pleasure." He said Henry excelled at having a good time. "It attracted everyone to him." Jefferson made these grumpy comments many years later as an old man. He had been a shy teenager when Henry was a popular adult.

"Mr. Henry had a little before broken up his store—or,

rather, it had broken him up; but his misfortunes were not traced, either in his [face] or conduct," Jefferson recalled. If Henry was sad, he didn't let people see it.

Still, he had been thinking. He could not make a living farming or storekeeping. What else could a person do in Hanover County to support a growing family? More importantly, what could Patrick Henry do well? He could talk.

What jobs called for a good talker? The ministry, teaching, and law. To be a teacher or a minister, a person had to go to college. Henry did not have the time or interest for years of study. So Patrick Henry decided to become a lawyer.

The French and Indian War found the colonists and English on the same side.

PATRICK
TAKES A TEST

—2—

On a clear April day in 1760, a tall backwoodsman rode into Williamsburg, capital of colonial Virginia. His wrinkled clothes were spattered with red mud from the roads he had ridden on on horseback from Hanover. Patrick Henry had come to the capital to get a license to practice law. Four of the colony's finest lawyers had agreed to test him.

Patrick Henry knew very little law just then. Some accounts—among them Jefferson's—say Henry spent only six weeks studying two law books before he rode to Williamsburg. At most, he studied six to eight months.

Yet Henry knew a lot about what happened in courts. Six of the twelve justices of the Hanover courts were his relatives, among them his half brother John Syme and his father John Henry. The courthouse was across the street from the Hanover Tavern where Patrick and Sarah lived. Most people in town sat in to watch interesting cases.

Patrick had listened to many legal arguments, and he always learned best by listening.

So here was Patrick Henry, ready to be tested on the law. John Randolph, king's lawyer for the colony, quizzed him for several hours. Henry could not name particular laws. He could not tell how a certain case had been decided. But he could argue from logic and history with great force.

Henry admitted cheerfully that he needed to study more. Randolph was *not* impressed with Henry's legal knowledge, but he *was* impressed by his brain. Randolph pointed to a pile of law books.

"You have never seen these books," said Randolph, "yet you are right and I am wrong. Mr. Henry, if your industry be only half equal to your genius, I predict you will do well. . . ." After Henry promised to study more, Randolph signed his license to practice law.

Henry read law for several months. Then he began getting cases, mostly from his or Sarah's many relatives. Meanwhile, he and Sarah still lived at the tavern her father owned. Henry was perfectly willing to serve customers or play the fiddle for guests.

Most of the time, however, he was off at court somewhere. He argued cases in six counties—Hanover, Goochland, Louisa, Albemarle, Chesterfield, and Cumberland. He would ride 100 miles (160 km) or more to a distant court. Or he might walk fifteen miles (54 km) to a courthouse. He never lost his love of the outdoors. If he walked, he could hunt along the way.

Henry had plenty of work. Yet it was just as hard for a lawyer to collect his bills as it was for a shopkeeper. Lots of his cases involved people trying to collect their own debts. In his second year of law, clients owed him £200, but paid only about £55. By 1763, Henry earned fees of £600, but was able to collect only £200.

This may sound like a tiny income, but £200 was a great sum of money in the 1760s. A tutor earned about £40 a year. The president of the College of William and Mary got £200 a year. For that sum, he not only ran the college, but he also served as pastor of a church.

Henry did so well because he won cases. He had a way of getting jury members to agree with his side. He knew most of them. Those he did not know, he studied carefully. When talking to a jury, he started slowly as if he were unsure of himself. In fact, he was testing how the jury took what he said. He watched faces and hands.

Once he got the feel of his audience, his deep-set blue eyes began to gleam. They were startling eyes, eyes that one of his daughters said were as blue as the sky on a perfectly cloudless day. Although he was always courteous in court, Henry would often set the room to laughing—if it helped his client.

In later years, Jefferson claimed that as a young man Henry was lazy. Yet, in his first three years as a lawyer, Henry took on 1,185 cases. That is about a case a day in courts spread over six counties. By 1764 he was doing so well that he could lend his father money. By 1767 he was lending to Sarah's dad. Henry began buying land, lots of land.

He and Sarah moved often. Every couple of years they moved to another place. They needed bigger houses because the family kept growing. Patrick and Sarah had three sons and three daughters. By the time the last was born, Patrick Henry's name was known throughout Virginia because of a famous court case and a famous speech.

THE PARSON'S CAUSE

— 3 —

The eight rows of oak benches in the Hanover court were already filled, and people leaned against the walls. Outside, those who had arrived late hunted for a place to hitch a horse or leave a wagon.

The leaves had fallen, but winter hadn't really set in yet on December 1, 1763. Some of the crowd outside shouted to Patrick Henry as he neared the packed courthouse. He spotted the arriving carriage of his uncle, the Reverend Patrick Henry.

"Sir, I'm sorry to see you here," said the young man.

"Why so?" asked his uncle.

"Because, sir, you know that I have never yet spoken in public. I fear that I shall be too overawed by your presence to be able to do my duty to my clients. Besides, sir, I shall have to say some hard things of the clergy, and I am very unwilling to give pain to your feelings," the younger man said.

Parson Henry shook his head. He said Patrick should not have taken this case. Still, if it made Patrick uneasy to have him there, he would leave. Parson Henry drove away.

Though the Reverend Patrick Henry left, twenty other ministers sat front and center inside. They had a stake in this case. The case was brought by the Reverend James Maury, Jefferson's one-time teacher. He was trying to force the tax collectors of Louisa County to give him more pay. The reason was an old law.

Under this old law, every Virginia parish had to pay its Anglican minister a certain amount of tobacco a year. Every taxpayer had to pay a share. In years when tobacco sold for high prices, ministers did well. When tobacco prices fell, ministers earned less.

One year the price of tobacco went so high that the ministers' pay would have been worth a small fortune, about £400. The Virginia House of Burgesses thought that was too much to pay ministers. The Burgesses passed a law that parishes should pay in money instead of in tobacco. They set a rate of two pennies per hundred pounds of tobacco, so the law was called the Two Penny Act.

The Act was very popular because it saved taxpayers a lot of money. It was especially popular in western Virginia. There, many people went to other churches, yet they still had to pay the salaries of Anglican ministers.

Taxpayers felt angry when ministers found a way to get rid of the law. The ministers got the English king to strike down the Two Penny Act. Once the law was set aside, ministers all over Virginia went to court. They asked for the extra pay they had not received.

Parson Maury's was the first case to reach the final stages. So far, things looked very good for the ministers.

The court had already ruled that Parson Maury should get the difference between what he had been paid in cash and the value of tobacco at the time. Since the case seemed to be lost, the lawyer for the county had dropped out. At the last minute, the county asked Patrick Henry to step in. He was good with juries. And it couldn't have hurt that the judge was his father.

As the new trial began, Judge John Henry wondered how Patrick, who had failed at so many things, would do. Head down, eyes downcast and nearly hidden, young Henry stumbled over his opening words. Judge Henry slumped in his seat. He felt embarrassed that his son was doing so poorly. The twenty parsons beamed. Once Maury won this case, their own chances for collecting back pay would be excellent.

Then the ministers stopped smiling as Henry's head came up and his shoulders straightened. No longer stooping, he rose to his full height. His intense blue eyes flashed toward the jury. His deep voice rose and fell, washing across the room. It invited first a chuckle, then a gasp of shock. The voice dripped with scorn or blazed with anger.

No one shuffled; no one coughed or rustled. The crowd leaned forward, caught in the spell of a master orator. No one in the room had ever heard such a speech. Tears rolled down Judge Henry's cheeks as his twenty-seven-year-old son spoke.

Henry talked of the proper role of government and the proper role of the church. In fact, he was not really talking about this case at all. He raised much larger issues. He spoke of these issues in a way ordinary people could understand.

He attacked the very concept of a church set up by governments. He attacked the whole idea that England could set aside laws voted by the colony's elected leaders. With bitter scorn, he reminded the jury that the parsons had turned to England to upset a law passed by the elected representatives of Virginia.

And, he purred, what is the reason for having an "established" clergy? The ministers were supposed to get people to obey laws. Yet the parsons refused to obey the Two Penny Law. By refusing to obey the law, these parsons were not filling their proper role, he said.

"Instead of useful members of the state, they ought to be considered as enemies of the community," he declared. If parsons didn't do their duty, "the community has no further need of their ministry, and may justly strip them of their jobs," he said.

"Do you want to rivet the chains of bondage on your own necks?" he demanded. If not, the jury should make an example of Parson Maury. It would be a warning not to oppose laws passed by "the only authority which could give them force, the government of the colony itself."

No wonder Henry didn't want his uncle, whom he admired, to hear what he had to say! Henry called the parsons rapacious (fiercely greedy) harpies. He said these greedy parsons did not worry about feeding and clothing the poor. Instead, they worried about their own pay.

He said these greedy parsons had gone over the heads of elected colonial leaders to appeal to England. The English king had no right to set aside laws passed by the colony's elected leaders, roared Henry.

Why, he said, a king who sets aside good laws like this one was not the father of his people. He had become a tyrant who "forfeits all right to his subject's obedience."

Maury's lawyer, all 300 pounds (145 kg) of him, heaved

*Henry arguing against
the parson's cause*

himself to his feet. "The gentleman has spoken treason," he shouted. All twenty ministers also were on their feet, arguing. Then they stomped out the door.

Most of the crowd chuckled broadly. Mr. Henry sure was telling those uppity parsons and that king a thing or two.

Henry urged the jury to make an example of Parson Maury. He said they had to award him *some* money but. . . . He paused and grinned. The jury, and the jury alone, could decide how much. Why, the jury could even decide that Parson Maury wasn't worth more than a farthing (less than a penny).

In less than five minutes the jury gave its verdict: one farthing. The amount was a flat insult to Parson Maury. The crowd cheered. People lifted Henry to their shoulders and paraded him in triumph around the courtyard.

Patrick Henry had attacked both the English church and the English government. The case came to be called the Parson's Cause. It was one of the first clear calls for keeping church and government separate. It was also the first step in Henry's career as the voice of colonial revolt against England. The revolt was not yet simmering, but the Parson's Cause marked Henry as a young man to watch.

"IF THIS
BE TREASON . . ."

—4—

The day, May 29, 1765, happened to be Henry's twenty-ninth birthday. A few days earlier, he had taken a seat from Louisa County in the Virginia House of Burgesses. The House of Burgesses was the lower house of the Virginia Assembly.

Henry got elected from Louisa County even though he lived in Hanover. He was making enough money in his law practice to buy land in Louisa. As a landowner, he could be elected even if he did not live there.

Here was Patrick Henry in the fine brick capitol where the Assembly made laws for the colony. A visitor could guess where most members lived by how they dressed. Tidewater men wore lace-trimmed satin or silk waistcoats and silk stockings. Some powdered their hair in the English fashion. Men from west of the Fall Line dressed more simply. They might even show up in boots and buckskins.

Not many of the finely dressed gentlemen paid much attention to the skinny and plainly dressed young fellow from Louisa. They were busy talking about that terrible law the English had dreamed up to squeeze money from the colonies.

News of the stamp tax reached Virginia shortly after Henry was elected. The Stamp Act taxed nearly every piece of paper in the colonies. Lawyers were supposed to pay a tax on every legal document they prepared. Even a deck of cards was to carry a tax. The tax had not gone into effect yet, but people were complaining hotly about it. Yet no one had dared speak out publicly.

New members of the Burgesses were supposed to sit politely for their first few weeks. They were expected to listen with respect to more experienced members. Henry had been in the Burgesses for nine days. He was the newest and youngest member. Yet it looked as if no one else had the gumption to speak out against this terrible tax. Henry stood up.

He moved that the House consider what Virginia should do about the Stamp Tax. He held a page ripped from a blank notebook. On it he had written some Resolves, statements that he wanted the Assembly to pass.

No official record exists of what he said. Fortunately, twenty-two-year-old Jefferson happened to be standing in the doorway. He later wrote about it. He said he heard "torrents of sublime oratory," floods of powerful speaking. He also heard one of the first speeches on the path to the American Revolution.

The first four Resolves Henry wanted passed were ideas colonists had talked about before. He said that when ex-

*Addressing the Virginia Assembly,
Henry was a formidable speaker.*

plorers and colonists came to America from England, they brought with them all their rights as English citizens. Two royal charters to Virginia later promised these same rights to colonists, he said.

People nodded. These first two Resolves were fine. The new fellow wasn't saying anything they could not accept. Then Henry got to the Third Resolve. He wanted the Burgesses to say "that the taxation of the people by themselves or by persons chosen by themselves . . . is the mark of British freedom. . . ."

The Fourth Resolve said that the people of Virginia had always paid taxes voted by their own Assembly. In other words, they only paid taxes that had been voted in Virginia.

Henry still had not said anything outrageous. Yet the way he spoke lured a growing crowd to the doors. Jefferson managed to keep his place. His sandy eyebrows shot up when he heard Henry state in bold tones:

> The General Assembly of this colony have the *sole* right and power to lay taxes on the people of this colony. Any attempt to take away that power has a tendency to destroy British as well as American freedom.

The buzz in the room rose to a roar. Why, that new fellow was saying that Virginians did not have to obey any tax law that they had not voted for themselves. Supporters of the crown leaped to their feet. They couldn't let such wild statements stand. Who was this hotheaded madman? One by one, they slammed into his ideas. They said terrible things about him. Some even threatened him. That didn't bother Henry. He just argued right back.

It is hard to show on a printed page how Henry spoke. The pace of his words, the tone, and the way he used his body were as important as the words he used. Like a great actor, his timing and his voice were as important as what he said.

"Caesar had his Brutus," he said, pausing to let that sink in. Everyone in the room had read Roman history. They knew that Brutus killed a Roman Emperor.

"Charles I had his Cromwell. . . ." Another pause let them recall how Oliver Cromwell had toppled a king of England.

"And George the Third . . ."

Before he could continue, the Speaker of the House shouted, "Treason! Treason!" George III was the king of England. Was the gentleman from Louisa suggesting that the king be killed?

Cleverly, Henry ended his sentence in a way few could criticize: ". . . may profit from their example." But then he boomed in a voice that reached beyond the open doors: "If this be treason, make the most of it!"

All five Resolves passed, although the last one, the bombshell, squeaked by with just one vote. Henry's speech opened the fight that ended the Stamp Act. He was the first in the colonies to speak out publicly against the tax law after it was passed. Soon, other colonies also took stands against the tax.

Within months, feelings were so strong against the tax that no one would take the unpopular job of selling the tax stamps. Leaders of the colonies decided to meet to talk about opposition to the Stamp Act. The Stamp Act Congress was the first general meeting of colonial leaders.

Henry normally was very modest. He didn't brag about what he had done. He didn't usually write down his own account of important events to be sure history got his role straight. Yet he did leave notes about his Stamp Act speech. He seems to have considered it the most important thing he ever did.

> The alarm spread throughout America with astonishing quickness. . . . The great point of resistance to British taxation was . . . established in the colonies. This brought on the war which finally separated the two countries and gave independence to ours.

After his great speech, Henry did not hang around Williamsburg basking in glory. He had law cases to try and lands to oversee. One day after his Stamp Act speech, Henry walked down the dusty main street of Williamsburg talking to a friend. He wore buckskin trousers and carried his saddle bags over his arm. Trailing behind him was the scrawny horse he planned to ride on the 80 mile (128 km) trip home. He wanted to check on the new house he was building.

PRIVATE TRAGEDY
IN A
CRITICAL TIME

5

For the next ten years, it wasn't always easy to find Patrick Henry. He might be arguing a court case in any of a dozen counties. He might be out west, looking at land. Or he might be at the General Assembly in Williamsburg.

Not long after his Stamp Act speech, the Henrys moved to a four-room house in Louisa County. The farm stood at the edge of the wilderness, on a road leading west. With Patrick gone so much, Sarah was often lonely. She was alone in an isolated house with young children and a few slaves.

Henry kept getting elected to the House of Burgesses. Yet he was so busy that he didn't always get to Williamsburg for the Assembly. It seemed as if everyone wanted Mr. Henry as his lawyer. Voters did not hold it against him that he skipped meetings of the Burgesses. In fact, both Louisa County and Hanover wanted to elect him.

In 1771, he told Sarah that they were going back to

Hanover. She was pleased to move closer to civilization. Now she'd get to see her family more. And the plantation they bought, Scotchtown, was a genuine estate! Scotchtown had a sixteen-room mansion and 1000 acres (400 ha) of land. Around the main house were enough buildings to resemble a little village. Scotchtown had its own schoolhouse, a blacksmith, an office, and warehouses.

The children loved it. Henry bought new horses and saddles for the older girls, and urged them to invite friends over. Henry's children adored him. He thought the little ones should be free to roam outdoors, as he did as a child. They didn't wear shoes until they were six or seven. He didn't send them to school until they were much older, sometimes as old as thirteen.

Yet Scotchtown hid a tragedy. Henry's wife was slipping into insanity. After the birth of her sixth child, her health failed and her mind wandered.

The first insane asylum in Virginia had opened a few years earlier, but it was a horrible place. A kind-hearted person like Patrick Henry would not send his wife there. Sixteen-year-old Patsy said she could manage the house and younger children.

By 1772 Mrs. Henry had to be locked up. She had to be tied into a special dress that kept her arms pinned down. Otherwise, she would have hurt herself or others. The younger children rarely saw her. When he was home, Henry spent hours with Sarah. He spoon-fed meals to her. When he was away, a black woman looked after Sarah in a basement room.

The woman who took care of Sarah Henry was a slave. Like other leading Virginians, Patrick Henry owned slaves. Yet

he hated the slave trade. In a letter written in 1773, he said he didn't see how Christians could support the slave trade. It is "against humanity, against the Bible, and destroys liberty."

"I believe a time will come when an opportunity will be offered to end this evil. Let us pass on to our children, together with our slaves, a pity for their unhappy lot, and a hatred of slavery." He added that slavery harmed whites as well as blacks. Though he said he hated slavery, he used their labor all his life. When he died, Patrick Henry owned sixty-seven slaves.

Yet he did not think the use of slaves was good for Virginia. In the same letter, he wrote: "How comes it that the lands in Pennsylvania are five times the value of ours?" he asked. He said it was because in Pennsylvania most farmers didn't use slaves, and because they could follow their own religion. Freedom attracts hardworking people, said Henry.

He felt strongly that people should be free to choose their own church. Yet Virginia had a church set up by the English government. Henry went to the established church. Although it suited him, he didn't think anyone should have to support one particular church. Yet ministers of Baptist, Presbyterian, and other churches were sometimes jailed for preaching. Some had to pay heavy fines.

Many jailed ministers asked Patrick Henry to defend them. Again and again, he talked juries into freeing them

The Henry plantation at Scotchtown

or cutting their fines. He would ride through rain squalls or snowstorms to defend a minister.

"They were so fortunate as to interest in their behalf the celebrated Patrick Henry," wrote a historian of Baptists in Virginia. "Being always a friend of liberty, he only needed to be told of their oppression. Without hesitation he stepped forward to their relief."

Helping the new church groups made him even more popular in western counties. More and more new settlers belonged to the new churches. They looked on Henry as their defender in court and their voice in the colonial Assembly.

Backcountry people also liked him because he agreed with them about opening the frontier. A 1763 Proclamation Law ordered colonists to stay out of lands west of the Alleghenies. Many settlers ignored the English law. Patrick, his father, and his father-in-law all bought land past the mountains. In fact, Henry held land claims as far west as the Mississippi River.

Henry was becoming prosperous. He had a lot to lose. Yet he thought that the colonies had to stand up to the English. There was no other way to protect people's liberties. And so, though his wife was so ill, Henry took the lead against English efforts to control the restless colony of Virginia.

By 1773, the new royal governor, Lord Dunmore, did not trust the House of Burgesses. And most of the members of the Burgesses did not trust Lord Dunmore. Several times, the governor had closed the Burgesses. He hoped its members would go home. If they were not meeting, they could not stir up more trouble for England.

Still, only the Burgesses could vote taxes. So the governor had to let them meet sometimes. Yet when the House of Burgesses met, Patrick Henry and other "hotheads" also gathered privately. They met behind closed doors of the Apollo room of the Raleigh Tavern.

Patrick Henry argued that it was important that all of Virginia's leaders stick together in their quarrel with England. Jefferson called it a "harmony of the bold with the cautious." He said this agreement let them move forward "in undivided mass." And, said Jefferson, the man most responsible for keeping Virginia's leaders together at this time was Henry.

They agreed that it was just as important for the colonies to stick together against England. How could that be done? Often Virginians did not even know what was going on in Pennsylvania or Massachusetts. The group in the Apollo room made a plan. They would have the House of Burgesses name a new kind of committee. The committee would send letters to other colonies. They would ask for information about what the British were doing, and what the other colonies planned.

In March 1773, Jefferson's brother-in-law, Dabney Carr, stood up in the Burgesses. He urged Virginia to name a Committee of Correspondence. It would "obtain the most early and authentic intelligence of all such acts . . . of the British Parliament as may relate to the British colonies."

Then, as planned, Henry went into action. He stormed against the English government. Some listeners were so stirred that they rushed outside and ripped down the royal flag. Seeing the rush of people coming out of the building, some people thought the capitol was burning.

Henry did fire up the Burgesses enough to get them to

name a Committee of Correspondence. Of course, Henry was named to the committee. And, as expected, the governor was furious. He closed the Virginia Assembly again. He hoped the hotheads would go home.

Instead, members of the Committee of Correspondence met in the Apollo room. They began sending off letters. Soon, information came back from other colonies. The committee heard how the people of Boston were fighting a tax on tea. Bostonians dressed as Indians had dumped tea in the harbor.

A few months later, they heard that the British planned to punish Boston by closing the port there. The Assembly was meeting again in Williamsburg. Henry, Richard Henry Lee, and other Patriots gathered at the Apollo room. They made a plan that would show that Virginians stood behind the people of Boston. They wanted the Burgesses to set the day the Boston Port Act took effect as a day of public prayer and fasting. How could the governor object to prayers?

The Burgesses met the next day. Without a single No vote, the Burgesses set June 1, 1774, as a day of public prayer and fasting. As soon as Governor Dunmore realized what they were up to, he dismissed them again.

Just as promptly, twenty-five members strolled down the street to the Raleigh Tavern. They met around the long table in the Apollo room. They agreed to urge people to boycott, or refuse to buy, British goods. Henry had already started his own boycott. He planted flax to make linen and bought a loom for weaving cloth. His family would not have to buy English woolens.

More importantly, Henry and his friends urged the Committee of Correspondence to call for a general congress of the colonies. Messengers raced off to notify other colonies of the idea.

In these tense months before the Revolution, Henry spent days riding the dirt roads to and from Williamsburg. When it rained, the roads turned to red mud. In hot weather, dust churned up. Yet, as he rode, Henry always noted the songs of birds and the amazing beauty of the countryside. He was determined that Virginia's own people would decide how to run that country.

In the muggy August heat of 1774, Henry rode to a special meeting of leaders of all Virginia counties. The group voted not to buy any English goods. They also voted not to import more slaves into America.

Then the Virginia Convention picked seven delegates, one of whom was Patrick Henry. These people would speak for Virginia at the first Continental Congress. Once again, Henry rode home. He had a lot to do before he could go to Philadelphia in September!

"I AM
AN AMERICAN"

—6—

Before the sun had burned off the morning mist, Henry rode out of Hanover on August 29, 1774. He had been home just three weeks. Now he guided his horse along narrow forest trails to Caroline County. There, he stopped to pick up Edmund Pendleton. The two disagreed often. Pendleton was careful and cautious, while Henry was ready to move boldly.

After two days, they reached Mount Vernon, home of Martha and George Washington. They talked all through dinner and into the evening. The next morning, after a huge breakfast, Washington, Pendleton, and Henry saddled up for the trip to Philadelphia where the Continental Congress would meet. Martha stood at the door.

"I hope you will stand firm," she told her guests. "I know George will." She knew that they risked their safety by serving in the Continental Congress. The English could declare them traitors, and they could be hanged.

The three rode downhill to the Potomac River where they boarded a ferry to Maryland. Then they rode to Annapolis. Another boat took them across the Chesapeake Bay. The cool breeze off the water was a welcome relief from the fierce August sun. It was so hot that they rose before dawn each day and rode only until noon. Then they stopped for the day, to avoid the scorching afternoon heat.

As they traveled, others heading for Philadelphia joined them. Soon they were riding with delegates to the Congress from Maryland, Delaware, and North Carolina.

Six miles outside Philadelphia, a noisy welcoming party joined them. Dozens of people on horseback had trooped out to escort them. A company of riflemen swung into the line of march. A band appeared. To the sound of trumpets, fifes, and drums, Patrick Henry and the others rode into Philadelphia for the first Continental Congress.

Richard Henry Lee was already there. He and Henry hoped the Congress would take strong actions against the English. They soon met others who thought like them. The Virginians found that they agreed with Samuel and John Adams of Massachusetts. The groups from Virginia and Massachusetts decided to work together.

On September 5, Congress opened in the new Carpenter's Hall. There had never been such a meeting. What rules should be followed? How should votes be taken? Should each colony have one vote, or should colonies with more people get more votes? Virginia was the biggest colony and had the most people. Should Virginia get more votes than a small colony? At first, Henry thought that sounded fair. Yet when smaller colonies objected, he changed his mind.

Henry gave his reasons in a speech. He pointed out

Opposite: Patrick Henry, George Washington, and Edmund Pendleton riding to the Continental Congress in Philadelphia. Above: the meeting of the Continental Congress

that British troops were camped in Boston. British warships were anchored in colonial ports. Courts all through the colonies had closed because of the unrest. He said the old government of the colonies had ended. In this time of crisis, it was vitally important for the colonies to stand together. People had to think and act in new ways.

"The distinctions between Virginians, Pennsylvanians, New Yorkers, and New Englanders are no more," he said. Then he used a phrase that stuck in people's memories. "I am not a Virginian, but an American." An American. That had a fine ring. Henry was asking the people of all colonies to act together as one people.

The delegates had promised to keep their meetings secret. No reporters wrote down what was said. Yet most remembered Henry's words. "I am an American" was a bold new idea.

Before the first Continental Congress ended, John Adams got a letter from a friend. The letter said, "We must fight, if we can't otherwise rid ourselves of British taxation. . . ." Adams read the letter to Patrick Henry. At the words, "we must fight," Henry nodded.

"By God, I am of that man's mind." Henry never swore. He was making a very solemn statement.

October had almost ended before Congress closed. Henry was eager to get home. Sarah was very sick. He needed to supervise the farm and check on the children.

Henry was a passionate speaker.

He also wanted to begin getting Virginia ready for possible war. As soon as he reached Hanover, Henry called volunteers together to form a militia company. The Hanover Volunteers drilled with two weapons: rifles and tomahawks.

A friend asked Henry if Great Britain would drive the colonies to violent action. Would there be war? Henry looked around to see who might be listening. Then he said, yes, he thought it might come to war.

"But do you think, Mr. Henry," the friend asked, "that an infant nation as we are, without . . . ammunition, ships of war or money . . . do you think it possible . . . to oppose successfully the fleets and armies of Great Britain?"

"I will be candid with you," Henry answered. "I doubt whether we will be able, alone, to cope with so powerful a nation. But," he paused, "where is France? Where is Spain? Where is Holland?" He named countries that were enemies of England. "Where will they be all this while? Do you suppose they will stand by, idle and indifferent spectators to the contest?"

Governor Dunmore might think Patrick Henry was a hothead. Yet he was a very practical rebel. He felt it was just as important to get help from other countries as it was to arm and train an army at home.

"GIVE ME LIBERTY
OR GIVE ME DEATH"

7

Henry didn't have far to ride to reach Richmond. Some Virginia leaders had to travel for a week over muddy spring roads to get there. They met in Richmond to keep away from Governor Dunmore. Richmond was far up the James River, at the Fall Line. Meeting there kept Patriot leaders away from the British warship that was anchored off Williamsburg. If the governor decided to order British marines to arrest colonial leaders, they would have plenty of warning ahead of time.

Delegates to the Virginia Convention met in the town's biggest building, St. John's Church. Thomas Jefferson and George Washington were there. So was every other important leader of the colony.

After three days, Henry felt restless and impatient. No one was saying anything new. People acted timid. He wasn't about to sit there doing nothing. The English had regiments of troops in Boston! They were trying to force colonists to pay unjust taxes. The English were taking away colonial rights and liberties. What was Virginia going to do? How could the biggest colony of all guard its liberty? Henry decided to force the convention to answer these questions.

He was thirty-nine years old in March of 1775. He had crushing personal problems. It is possible that his wife had just died. The exact facts are not known. Sarah Henry died in the early spring of 1775, but the date is not recorded. Henry did not talk about his personal grief. He put all his energies into the struggle with Britain.

On March 23, it was warm enough that the windows could be left open. Those who couldn't squeeze inside the church listened at the windows. At first Henry spoke softly. People outside could barely hear. He said that Virginia must form its own militia. If the colony had volunteer soldiers, England would not have a reason to keep a standing army in the colony.

"Resolved, therefore, that this colony be immediately put into a state of defense."

Timid people understood instantly what Henry was up to. He was trying to arm Virginia for war. Cautious people argued hotly against any action that would anger the British. They said Mr. Henry's ideas were too bold, too rash. They said it was too soon for such steps. The colony should ask the English politely to end bad laws.

Quietly, Henry defended his plan. He spoke with respect to those who did not agree with him. He said he knew that everyone in the room was a patriot. He understood that worthy gentlemen might see the same subject in a different light.

But, he insisted, the question was one of freedom or slavery. Why were there armed fleets in our ports? Why were British troops drilling in Boston? Do not be fooled, he warned. The British had put ships and soldiers among us to make us back down. They did not send troops and ships because they loved the colonies.

"And what have we to oppose to them? Shall we try argument?" He paused. "We have been trying that for the last ten years. Have we nothing new to offer upon the subject?"

"Shall we beg England yet again to listen to us?" he asked scornfully. "We have done that many times," he said. "We have sent petitions. We have asked humbly."

"We have done everything that could be done to avert the storm which is now coming on."

Henry built his case slowly to show how reasonable and patient the colonies had been. His voice rose as he told all the ways the colonists had begged the king to listen: "We have petitioned—we have remonstrated—we have supplicated—we have prostrated ourselves before the throne . . ." People could almost see colonists stretched out on the floor begging before a fat English king.

"Our petitions have been slighted." He said every petition or other message had been met with scorn and violence. "We have been insulted again and again."

"If we wish to be free—if we mean to preserve . . . those . . . privileges for which we have [fought] . . . we must fight! I repeat it, sir, we must fight."

Henry was saying openly what only a few had talked of privately. The colonies must go to war with England. As he reached the end of his speech, Henry's whole body spoke for him.

"They tell us . . . that we are weak," he said. His head hung down, his body drooped. "But when shall we be

"Give me liberty or give me death"
—the speech for which Henry
is best remembered

stronger? Will it be the next week, or the next year? Will it be when we are totally disarmed, and when a British guard shall be stationed in every house?"

"Our chains are forged," he said. "They may be heard clanking on the plains of Boston!" His shoulders slumped. His hands were crossed in front of him as if heavy chains weighed down his wrists. He drooped like a chained slave, crushed with the weight of his bonds. In this way, he created an image of the colonies as beaten, pitiful slaves.

Then his voice surged with new power. "The war is inevitable—and let it come. I repeat . . . let it come."

His head went up. His shoulders squared. He seemed to fling away the unseen chains that had weighed him down. He stood tall, proud, and free. His voice rang through the room and out the open windows.

"Gentlemen may cry peace, peace—but there is no peace. . . . The war is actually begun!

"The next gale that sweeps from the north will bring to our ears the clash of . . . arms!

"Our brethren are already in the field! Why stand we here idle? What is it that gentlemen wish?"

Then came some of the most quoted words in American history: "Is life so dear, or peace so sweet, as to be purchased at the price of chains and slavery? Forbid it, Almighty God!" He stretched his arms over his head. The muscles in his neck bulged as he stretched upward.

"I know not what course others may take; but as for me . . . give me liberty or give me death!"

As he said "give me liberty," he waved an ivory letter opener. At "give me death," he pretended to stab himself.

For a few minutes, the audience was too stunned to act. Then Richard Henry Lee and Jefferson stepped forward.

They supported Henry's argument. Virginians must take arms, they said. By a close vote, the Convention agreed. Delegates voted to form a militia and chose Henry to head a committee to make plans. He didn't waste any time. One day later, the plan for a militia in every county was ready.

The convention had one more piece of business. It re-elected Henry and six others to go back to Philadelphia for the Second Continental Congress.

Before he left for Philadelphia again, Henry could note with pride that militia units were forming all through the colony. One group wore "Liberty or Death" printed across their shirts.

THE GUNPOWDER
MARCH

8

Orders came from London to colonial governors. Seize all gunpowder in the colonies. Keep it out of the hands of possible rebels.

The Massachusetts royal governor sent British troops across the countryside to take gunpowder stored in Concord. This move led to fighting at Lexington and Concord. Minute Men battled British troops to save their arms and gunpowder.

At almost the same time, Virginia's Governor Dunmore decided to take Williamsburg's gunpowder secretly. The powder belonged to the whole community. For safety, it was stored in an eight-sided brick building called the Powder Magazine. The marines slipped into town during the dark of night. They loaded more than a dozen barrels of gunpowder onto a cart. Then they took it to a ship anchored in the James River.

The people of Williamsburg discovered the theft the

next morning. Was the governor trying to disarm them? How would they defend themselves in case of an emergency? Word of the seizure flashed through the countryside to Fredericksburg where new militia companies were drilling under George Washington. Hasty plans were made to retake the gunpowder.

Yet many people urged caution. They didn't want to risk starting a war. Some leaders of the colony went to the governor. He promised to return the powder sometime. Then Washington and other militia leaders agreed not to march on Williamsburg.

Henry didn't agree with the decision. He called the Hanover Volunteers to arm and to meet him May 2, 1775. About 150 armed men showed up. In a rousing speech, Henry vowed to lead an armed troop to Williamsburg. They would force the governor to give back the powder or pay for it. Would the Volunteers follow him? Their cheers answered him.

The small force headed for Williamsburg. As they traveled, more armed men joined them. Soon several hundred were marching to the colonial capital.

The governor panicked. He sent his wife and family to safety aboard a British ship. He passed out weapons to his slaves and ordered English marines to place cannons around the Governor's Palace. He warned citizens that if he or his staff were attacked or insulted, he would order Williamsburg shelled and burned to the ground.

The English governor,
Lord Dunmore

Henry had set off a crisis. The threat of burning alarmed townspeople. Most colonial leaders did not approve of his march. Who had given him the right to lead armed troops? Did he realize he might be starting a war?

Some leaders might think he was wrong, but as Henry neared the capital, crowds cheered him. Fifteen miles from Williamsburg, he halted his troop of several hundred volunteers. He sent a small group to demand that English officials pay £330 for the stolen gunpowder, twice its real cost. Frightened officials came back with a written promise to pay. Henry wrote out a receipt, saying he would turn the money over to the proper authorities.

The governor had backed down, but as soon as Henry's small army scattered, Dunmore got his courage back. On May 6, 1775, he issued a notice naming Patrick Henry an outlaw. It warned citizens to have nothing to do with him.

Henry was not particularly worried. He had hoped to stir people up to fight the British. He said that most people were not excited by talk of taxes on tea and such things.

"But tell them of the robbery on the Magazine [the place powder was stored] and that the next step will be to disarm them, you bring the subject home to [them], and they will be ready to fly to arms to defend themselves."

After the gunpowder march, Henry was more popular than ever. He was a hero. When he left for the second Continental Congress, militia from three counties rode with him to the Maryland border. They wanted to protect him in case Dunmore tried to arrest him.

Henry rode to Philadelphia sure that war was coming. Yet the Congress wasn't ready in 1775 to declare independence from England. About the only delegates who spoke openly of the idea were Samuel and John Adams, Patrick

By *the* LION *&* UNICORN, Dieu & mon droit, *their Lieutenant-Generals, Governours, Vice Admirals, &c. &c. &c. &c.*

A HUE & CRY.

WHEREAS I have been informed, from undoubted authority, that a certain PATRICK HENRY, of the county of Hanover, and a number of *deluded followers,* have taken up arms, chosen their officers, and, styling themselves an *independent company,* have marched out of their county, encamped, and put themselves in a posture of war; and have written and despatched letters to divers parts of the country, exciting the people to join in these *outrageous* and *rebellious* practices, to the *great terrour* of all his Majesty's *faithful* subjects, and in *open defiance* of *law* and *government ;* and have *committed other acts of violence,* particularly in *extorting* from his Majesty's *Receiver-General* the sum of 330 l. under *pretence* of *replacing the powder* I *thought proper* to order from the magazine; whence it undeniably appears, there is *no longer* the least security for the *life* or *property* of any man: Wherefore, I have *thought proper,* *with the advice of his Majesty's Council,* and *in his Majesty's name,* to issue this my proclamation, strictly charging *all persons,* upon their *allegiance,* not to *aid, abet,* or *give countenance* to the said PATRICK HENRY, or *any other persons* concerned in *such unwarrantable combinations;* but, on the contrary, to oppose *them,* and *their designs,* by *every means,* which designs must otherwise inevitably involve the *whole country* in the *most direful calamity,* as they will call for the *vengeance of offended Majesty,* and the *insulted laws,* to be *exerted here,* to vindicate the *constitutional* authority of government.

Given, *&c.* this 6th day of May, 1775.

D * * * * *.

G * * d * * * the P * * * * *.

The broadside (notice) Dunmore issued
naming Patrick Henry an outlaw

Henry, and a few others. The Congress did agree to name George Washington to command colonial troops outside Boston. That left Virginia without its best military leader.

Back home, Henry was picked to lead the new First Regiment of Virginia. The post made him commander in chief of Virginia's Patriot forces. He had no experience as a soldier. He had never been in a battle. Yet when news spread that Patrick Henry commanded the regiment, enlistments rose sharply. By October, Colonel Henry commanded about 1,000 recruits. Arms were so scarce that they were told to bring their squirrel guns along.

Governor Dunmore, by the way, had long since boarded a ship and left Williamsburg. He ordered British ships to attack other towns that were not so well defended.

Colonel Henry was very popular with his troops and officers. He wasn't much admired by other senior officers who had more military experience. They felt he was not strict enough with the troops. Even his friend Washington said Henry was no military leader.

"My countrymen made a mistake," Washington wrote, "when they took Henry out of the Senate to place him in the field; and pity it is that he does not see this, and [resign]."

Other officers hoped to replace Colonel Henry as commander. Some of them were political enemies who resented his popularity. Another person was named general, thus outranking Henry. Angered and hurt, he resigned in early 1776.

Even though he felt bitter, Henry did not hold grudges. He did not let his personal feelings cloud his patriotism. Before he left camp, he urged his officers to serve their new commanders loyally.

As he was about to leave, large groups of soldiers started milling around and shouting. They said if Patrick Henry was leaving camp, they were quitting the regiment. They had signed up because of Colonel Henry. If he left, they left, too. Henry stayed an extra night in Williamsburg to talk to the soldiers. He went from one tent to another, telling them they must not quit the Patriot cause. The struggle was much more important than one person.

Henry felt deeply unhappy, but there were important things to do. He had to get home to see how his daughter, Patsy, was managing the younger children. But he didn't expect to be home long. The colony faced almost certain war with England. John Adams wrote Henry from Massachusetts that each colony would have to form a new government. Henry began thinking about how that government should be shaped.

THE WAR
GOVERNOR

$$-9-$$

When the Continental Congress declared independence in 1776, Patrick Henry was not there. He was busy with another meeting in Virginia. Virginia's leaders were split between the two places. Some served in Philadelphia at the Congress. The rest met to plan Virginia's future.

On June 29, 1776, the Virginia meeting adopted a plan for a new state government. Then the same group chose the first governor of the new state. By a vote of 60 to 45, it was Patrick Henry.

Governor Henry had hardly taken the oath of office July 5, 1776, before he collapsed with fever. Many people in the coastal regions suffered from malaria. They didn't know then that the fever was spread by mosquitoes from low-lying swamps. Yet they knew that the highlands were healthier. The new governor went home to Hanover to recover. He was so sick that rumors spread that he had died. For five weeks, he was too weak to go back to Williamsburg. When he did return, he still wasn't completely recovered.

Henry took charge of a huge state. In 1776, Virginia claimed an area bigger than all of New England. It included all of what is now West Virginia and Kentucky, as well as lands that today are in Maryland, Pennsylvania, Ohio, Indiana, and Illinois. [See the map of Virginia on page 70.]

When Governor Henry started his new job, the frontier regions were under heavy Indian attack. Closer to home, he had a dozen equally urgent worries. He had to arm ships to patrol the coast against British warships. He needed to recruit more men for Washington's armies and for the militia. Washington wrote again and again of the desperate need for more soldiers, food, and guns.

Henry had a huge responsibility, but the governor had very little power. Governor Henry called the job a "mere phantom." The governor was saddled with a Council of eight, chosen by the House. He was not supposed to take any action without the Council's approval.

Even though he had little power and was often sick, Governor Henry got a great deal done. He was still very good at talking people into things. He used his gift of speech to convince the Council to agree to many of his plans.

The war went badly for the Patriot armies. Washington had lost many battles. Some people wanted to replace him as commander. Henry stayed fiercely loyal. When a group tried to get him to join them secretly in trying to dump Washington, Henry sent urgent warnings to the general.

Governor Henry got some able help in guarding the frontiers. A tall, red-haired, twenty-three-year old frontiersman

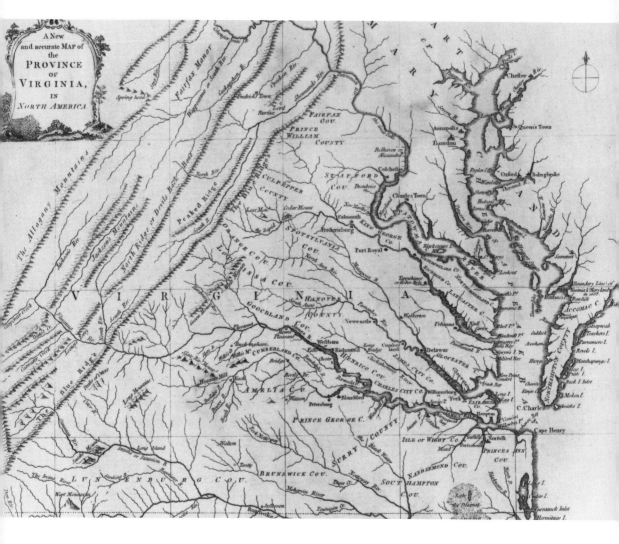

Above: a map of the state of Virginia.
Opposite: George Rogers Clark's wilderness
expedition helped save the Northwest
Territory from British hands.

from Kentucky came to see him. George Rogers Clark warned that Indian raids were destroying Kentucky settlements. He asked for gunpowder for Kentucky sharpshooters. Henry helped him get gunpowder needed to fight the Indians.

A year later Clark came back. This time he offered to lead frontiersmen to protect the huge northwest region. He said he would take a force hundreds of miles into the wilderness. He hoped to get all the way to the fort at Detroit. Again, Governor Henry backed him.

Fewer than 200 men, armed with flintlocks and tomahawks, headed toward the Illinois country. Under Clark's brilliant leadership, this tiny band fought off Indian attacks. They captured British outposts. They talked French settlements into backing the Patriot cause. Clark's efforts helped save the Northwest Territory from the British.

Meanwhile, Henry's first one-year term had ended. No one ran against him for a second and then a third term.

Partway into his second term, the governor brought a young bride to the Governor's Palace. Dorothea Dandridge was twenty years younger than her husband. She had been a toddler when Henry first met Jefferson at her parents' home in Hanover. "Dolly" Dandridge and Governor Henry were married October 9, 1777.

The Governor's Palace in Williamsburg, where Henry lived when he was governor of Virginia

When Dolly moved to the Governor's Palace, it was a bit of a homecoming. Dolly's grandfather had been a colonial governor of Virginia. Her mother was born in the Governor's Palace. A cousin of Martha Washington, Dolly was at home among the elegant folk of the Tidewater.

Her new husband worried constantly about the war with Britain. There was never enough time to do everything, or enough money to pay for urgently needed supplies. During the winter of 1777–78, Washington's troops were starving at Valley Forge. Governor Henry worked frantically to get food and clothes to Virginia regiments. When he could not buy supplies, he ordered state agents to seize food to send to the troops.

Under state law, a governor could not serve more than three terms in a row. Four years had to pass before a person could be elected again. Thomas Jefferson followed Patrick Henry as governor.

At about the same time, British forces closed in on the state. The task of organizing the defense of a huge state from British troops, raiders, and ships fell to Jefferson. Probably no governor could have done it. There weren't enough Patriot forces in Virginia to stop the British.

British forces captured Portsmouth, Richmond, and other key areas. One raiding party nearly got both Patrick Henry and Thomas Jefferson. They escaped when a Patriot captain overheard plans to capture state leaders. He galloped cross-country to warn them just in time.

Henry hoped his family would be safe at their new home. He had sold the Hanover place and moved to Henry County (named for him) in western Virginia. In 1780 he was elected to the Virginia House.

Meanwhile, the war news got worse. The British kept capturing more areas. Some people blamed the governor. A small group, including Patrick Henry, asked for an investigation of Governor Jefferson's actions. They said he had not done enough to defend the state.

After the war ended in 1783, the charges were dropped. Yet Jefferson never forgave Patrick Henry. For the rest of his life, he rarely had a good word to say about Henry. As time passed, the two split on many political questions. They almost never seemed to agree. Since Jefferson is so widely respected, his bad opinions have muddied the record of Patrick Henry's life.

Nothing dimmed Henry's popularity during his lifetime, however. In 1784 Henry was elected governor again. He served two terms, then decided not to run again. The malaria fever kept coming back. He was only fifty in 1786, but he felt like an old man. Yet his public career had not ended. He faced one more great battle over the form of the new United States government.

ONE LAST BATTLE

10

The setting sun spun a red glow on the horizon as a stooped man in dusty homespun clothes guided his two-wheeled open carriage into Richmond. Patrick Henry had come to the new state capital for the last great battle of his life.

The Revolution had been won. The United States was independent. Yet the new government did not work well. Washington and others thought a big change was needed or the union of states would fail.

A meeting had been called in 1787 to write a plan for a new government. Henry was elected to the Constitutional Convention, but refused to serve. The Convention had written a new Constitution, or basic set of laws, for the United States. Now Virginia had to decide whether to ratify, or approve, the plan.

James Madison had written a lot of the Constitution. He was worried, for he knew how persuasive Mr. Henry could be. He wrote to Jefferson: "The part which Mr. Henry will take is unknown here. Much will depend on it. I had taken it for granted . . . he would be in opposition. . . ." Madison said Henry was the person most likely to bring about the defeat of the Constitution.

The Virginia meeting opened June 2, 1788. The group agreed to have a shorthand reporter take down the debates. For the first time, Henry's speeches were recorded as he spoke. For three weeks he led the fight against the Constitution. There are 652 pages of printed accounts of speeches at the meeting. Of these, 136 pages record what Mr. Henry had to say. Even that record doesn't include it all. Sometimes the shorthand recorder got so interested in what was being said that he forgot to write it down.

Why did Henry fight so hard to defeat the Constitution? He knew that the government had to be made stronger. Yet he didn't want a government as strong as the one in this Constitution. He thought the Constitution made the central government far too powerful. He wanted to protect the power of states. He wanted the states to remain more important than the central government.

"What right had they [the group that wrote the Constitution] to say . . . 'We, the People,' instead of We, the States?" he demanded. Again and again he returned to this point. The Constitution reduced the role of states. He said the change would create one "great consolidated national government of the people of all the states." He feared the power of such a central government.

He was also worried about protecting the South. He feared that the fast-growing northern states would have too much say in how the government was run. The South might be outvoted in Congress. Years earlier, Patrick had said, "I am not a Virginian. I am American." In this argument, he spoke as a Virginian.

He also refused to support a Constitution that did not have a bill of rights to protect basic freedoms. The Virginia Constitution had a strong bill of rights, adopted in 1776, that Henry had helped shape. It protected freedom of speech and religion and other liberties. How could people be safe from a powerful government without a bill of rights, he demanded.

For three weeks he argued with all his skill against the Constitution. He called it the "most fatal plan that could possibly be conceived to enslave a free people." He feared a government that could raise armies and collect taxes directly instead of through the states.

Washington did not attend the debates. He had been chairman of the Constitutional Convention. He felt it was proper for him to stay out of the debate in Virginia. Yet he worked behind the scenes to win approval.

Leading those in favor of the Constitution was James Madison. Once described as so small that he wasn't as big as half a cake of soap, Madison was not a good speaker. Yet he knew every argument for or against the Constitution. He had helped write it. He and his allies met every argument Henry made.

Henry nearly swayed the Virginia vote against the Constitution. He did not succeed for many reasons. One of them was Washington. Everyone expected him to be the first president. People admired and trusted him. Also, eight states had already voted to join the Union. Could Virginia remain strong outside it?

Henry tried to get Virginia to insist that a bill of rights

be added *before* it ratified the Constitution. By a close vote, 88 to 80, his motion lost. Then the delegates voted, 89 to 79, to ratify the Constitution.

Henry had fought with all his skill against the Constitution. Yet even before the vote went against him, he promised to obey the law. He said if the new government was approved, he would be a loyal citizen. He said he would work peacefully and legally to make the changes he favored.

In one way, he did succeed. The Bill of Rights he had demanded was soon added as the first ten amendments to the Constitution.

Once Washington took office, Henry slowly came to accept the new government. He had always respected Washington. As the years passed, the strongest criticism of Washington's government came from Jefferson, who formed a new political party that opposed Washington. Washington and his supporters came to be called the Federalist Party. More and more, Patrick Henry sided with the Federalists.

President Washington offered Henry a whole string of jobs. He asked him to represent the United States in Spain. Henry was honored, but refused. Then the president asked him to be secretary of state. Next, President Washington asked him to become the chief justice of the U.S. Supreme Court. That was quite an offer for a person who once almost failed his law exams! Henry said he was too ill to travel.

He was also busy trying to earn money to support his still-growing family. In 1786, Governor Henry noted that Dorothea had "five very fine and promising children." Soon there were six more, or eleven from his second marriage plus six from his first.

Henry liked having children around. He would lie on

Henry died at his family home, Red Hill.

the floor and let the little ones crawl over him. Or he would saddle a horse and put one small child in front and one behind him for a short ride. Other times he played the fiddle while the children danced around him.

To make money to support his big family, Henry returned to the practice of law. He also kept on buying and selling land. Before he died, he was one of the one hundred largest property holders in Virginia.

In 1799, Washington asked him to run as a Federalist either for Congress or for the Virginia House. Henry agreed to stand for the Virginia House from Charlotte County, where the family now lived. He was elected easily. Charlotte was the fifth county to elect him to the Virginia House.

He never took office, though, because he was too ill. In June 1799, Patrick Henry died at his home, Red Hill, in Charlotte County. He was sixty-three.

When his will was found, it included a sealed envelope. Inside were notes for what he may have seen as his most important achievement. It was a copy of the Stamp Act Resolves he had offered on his twenty-ninth birthday years before.

FOR
FURTHER READING

Beeman, Richard R. *Patrick Henry: A Biography.* New York: McGraw Hill, 1974.

Bliven, Bruce Jr. *The American Revolution 1760–1783.* New York: Random House, 1958.

Campion, Nardi Reeder. *Patrick Henry, Firebrand of the Revolution.* Boston: Little Brown, 1961.

Dickinson, Alice. *The Stamp Act.* New York: Franklin Watts, 1970.

Fritz, Jean. *Where Was Patrick Henry on the 29th of May?* New York: Coward, McCann & Geoghagan, 1975.

Gill, Harold B., Jr., and Finlayson, Ann. *Colonial Virginia.* Nashville: Thomas Nelson, 1973.

Leckie, Robert. *The World Turned Upside Down: The Story of the American Revolution.* New York: G.P. Putnam, 1973.

Martin, Teri. *Patrick Henry, Patriot.* Philadelphia: Westminster Press, 1972.

Mayer, Henry. *Patrick Henry and the American Republic.* New York: Franklin Watts, 1986.

Morris, Richard B. *American Revolution.* New York: Franklin Watts, 1956.

Rubin, Louis Decimus. *Virginia: A History.* New York, Nashville: American Association for State and Local History/Norton, 1977.

BIBLIOGRAPHY

Beeman, Richard R. *Patrick Henry: A Biography*. New York: McGraw-Hill, 1974.

Bridenbaugh, Carl. *Seat of Empire: The Political Role of Eighteenth-Century Williamsburg*. New York: Holt, 1958.

Campbell, Norine Dickson. *Patrick Henry: Patriot & Statesman*. New York: Devin-Adair Co., 1969.

Dabney, Virginius. *Virginia: The New Dominium*. New York: Doubleday, 1971.

Goldman, Eric F. "Firebrands of the Revolutions," July, *National Geographic*. 1974: 13–19.

Hume, Ivor Noel. *1775: Another Part of the Field; A Month by Month Account of Events in Virginia*. New York: Alfred Knopf, 1966.

Jensen, Merrill. *The Founding of a Nation: A History of the American Revolution, 1763–1776*. New York: Oxford University Press, 1968.

Jordan, Daniel P. *Political Leadership in Jefferson's Virginia.* Charlottesville, Va.: University of Virginia Press, 1983.

Main, Jackson Turner. *The Antifederalists: Critics of the Constitution (1781–1788).* Chapel Hill, N.C.: University of North Carolina Press, 1961. Published for the Institute of Early American History and Culture at Williamsburg.

Meade, Robert Douthat. *Patrick Henry: Patriot in the Making.* Vol. 1. Philadelphia: Lippincott Co., 1957.

———. *Patrick Henry: Practical Revolutionary.* Vol. 2. Lippincott. 1969.

Rouse, Parke. *Planters & Pioneers: Life in Colonial Virginia.* New York: Hastings House, 1968.

Rubin, Louis Decimus. *Virginia: A History.* New York: Norton, 1977.

Smith, Page. *A New Age Now Begins: A People's History of the American Revolution,* Vols. 1 & 2. New York: McGraw Hill, 1976.

Tyler, Moses Coit. *Patrick Henry.* 1898 Reprint. American Statesman Series. New York: Chelsea House, 1980.

Umbreit, Kenneth. *Founding Fathers: Men Who Shaped Our Traditions.* New York: Harper Brothers, 1941.

Willison, George F. *Patrick Henry and His World.* Garden City, N.Y.: Doubleday, 1969.

SOURCE NOTES

Note that only statements made by Patrick Henry at the Virginia ratifying convention in 1788 are direct quotations. All other quotations from his speeches are reconstructions, and sources vary somewhat on the exact wording. Most sources use a three-volume history by a grandson, William Wirt Henry.

INTRODUCTION
"He has only to say . . ." Umbreit, p. 200
"I think he was the . . ." Campbell, pp. 63–4
". . . a real half Quaker . . ." Meade, Vol. 1. p. 179
"He left us all far behind . . ." Willison, p. 9

CHAPTER 1
"His manners had . . ." Campbell, p. 22, modified quote
    (face for countenance)
"Mr. Henry had . . ." Campbell, p. 22

CHAPTER 2
"You have never seen . . ." Campbell, p. 25

CHAPTER 3
"Sir, I'm sorry . . ." Meade, Vol. 1, p. 128
"Instead of useful members . . ." Meade, Vol. 1. p. 133
"Do you . . ."
"the gentleman has spoken treason . . ." Willison, p. 80

CHAPTER 4
"that taxation . . ." Umbreit, p. 209
"The General Assembly have . . ." modified from Beeman,
      p. 36
"Caesar had his . . ." Meade, Vol. 1, p. 172+
"The alarm spread . . ." Beeman, p. 81–2, quoting William
      Wirt Henry

CHAPTER 5
"against humanity, against Bible" Willison, appendix
"I believe. . . ." Campbell, p. 100
"How comes it" Meade, Vol. 1, p. 386
"They were so fortunate . . ." Campbell, p. 101
"harmony of the bold . . ." Willison, p. 189
"obtain the most early . . ." Beeman, p. 49

CHAPTER 6
"I hope you will stand firm . . ." Meade, Vol. 1, p. 315
"The distinctions . . ." Smith, Vol. 1, p. 431
"We must fight . . ." Meade, Vol. 1, p. 333
"By god . . ."
"But do you think, Mr. Henry" Meade, Vol. 1, pp. 334–5

CHAPTER 7
"Resolved, therefore . . ." Meade, Vol. 2, p. 29
"And what have we to oppose . . ." Meade, Vol. 2, pp. 33–5

CHAPTER 8
"But tell them . . ." Willison, p. 275
"My countrymen . . ." Beeman, p. 77

CHAPTER 10
"the part which Mr. Henry . . ." Campbell, pp. 324–5
"What right had they . . ." Meade, Vol. 2, p. 350
"great consolidated government . . ." Willison, p. 418

INDEX

ABOUT
THE AUTHOR

Diana Reische is a freelance writer and editor who specializes in history and social studies materials for in-school use. The former National Affairs editor of *Senior Scholastic* magazine, she has written and edited American high school, junior high, and upper elementary history and government textbooks for Prentice-Hall, Scholastic, Ginn, and other publishers. The author of several local and specialized histories, Ms. Reische recently completed a biography for young people of John and Abigail Adams. She is currently at work on a book on citizenship education.

In addition to history, Ms. Reische's interests are art, ballet, skiing, and efforts to protect the environment. Ms. Reische is married to a stockbroker and has two college-age sons.